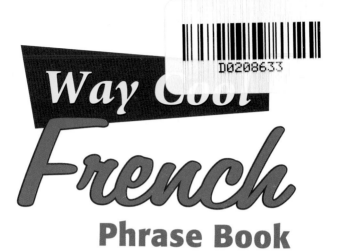

Way Cool *French*

Phrase Book

Third Edition

JANE WIGHTWICK

New York Chicago San Francisco Lisbon London Madrid Mexico City
Milan New Delhi San Juan Seoul Singapore Sydney Toronto

About this book

Jane Wightwick
had the idea

Wina Gunn
wrote the pages

Leila & Zeinah Gaafar
(aged 10 and 12) drew the
first pictures in
each chapter

Robert Bowers
(aged 52) drew the other
pictures, and designed
the book

Marie-Claude Dunleavy did the
French stuff (with some help
from Alix Fontaine)

Important things that
must be included

ISBN 978-0-07-180739-5
MHID 0-07-180739-X

e-ISBN 978-0-07-180740-1
e-MHID 0-07-180740-3

McGraw-Hill Education products are available at special quantity discounts to use as premiums and sales promotions or for use in corporate training programs. To contact a representative, please e-mail us at bulksales@mcgraw-hill.com.

This book is printed on acid-free paper.

Printed and bound by Tien Wah Press, Singapore.

This book features companion audio files available for download.
To access this material, visit McGraw-Hill Professional's Media Center at:
www.mhprofessional.com/mediacenter, then enter this book's ISBN and
your e-mail address. You will receive an e-mail message with a download
link for the additional content. This book's ISBN is: 0-07-180739-X.

What's inside

Making friends

How to be cool with the group

Wanna play?

Our guide to joining in everything from hide-and-seek to the latest electronic game

Feeling hungry

Order your favorite foods or go local

Looking good

Make sure you keep up with all those essential fashions

Hanging out

At the pool, beach, or theme park – don't miss out on the action

70

Pocket money

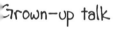

Spend it here!

90

Grown-up talk

blah!
blah!
blah!
blah!

If you really, really have to!

100

Extra stuff

All the handy things – numbers, months, time, days of the week

108

my big brother
mon grand frère
👄 mo gro frair

grandpa
papi
👄 pah-pee

grandma
mamie
👄 ma-mee

ad
pa
👄 pah-pah

mom
maman
👄 ma-mon

my little sister
ma petite sœur
👄 ma pteet sir

Half a step this way

stepfather/stepmother

beau-père/belle-mère

👄 bow pair/bel mair

stepbrother/stepsister

beau-frère/belle-sœur

👄 bow frair/bel sir

half brother/half sister

demi frère/demi sœur

👄 dumee frair/dumee sir

Hi!

Salut!

👄 saloo

What's your name?

Comment tu t'appelles?

👄 ko-mo too tapel

My name's ...

Je m'appelle ...

👄 jer mapel

8

Kissing is extremely popular among French children. You can't possibly say hello to your friends in the morning without kissing them on both cheeks. Try this in front of your mirror if your friends at home won't let you experiment on them.

Are you OK?
Ça va?
👄 sa va

Cool, and you?
Ça boume, et toi?
👄 sa boom, eh twa

Where are you from?
T'es d'où?
👄 tay doo?

from Canada

du Canada

👄 doo kana-da

from Ireland

d'Irlande

👄 deer-lond

from Scotland

d'Écosse

👄 day-cos

from Wales

du Pays de Galles

👄 doo pay-ee der gal

from the U.S.

des États-Unis

👄 days etaz-oo-nee

from England

d'Angleterre

👄 donglutair

Les textos

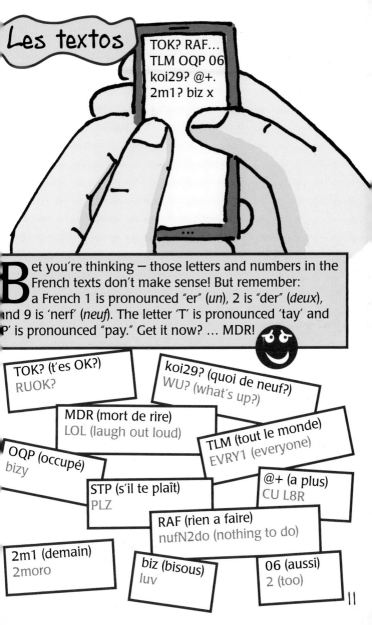

TOK? RAF...
TLM OQP 06
koi29? @+.
2m1? biz x

Bet you're thinking — those letters and numbers in the French texts don't make sense! But remember: a French 1 is pronounced "er" (*un*), 2 is "der" (*deux*), and 9 is 'nerf' (*neuf*). The letter 'T' is pronounced 'tay' and 'P' is pronounced "pay." Get it now? ... MDR!

TOK? (t'es OK?)
RUOK?

koi29? (quoi de neuf?)
WU? (what's up?)

MDR (mort de rire)
LOL (laugh out loud)

OQP (occupé)
bizy

TLM (tout le monde)
EVRY1 (everyone)

STP (s'il te plaît)
PLZ

@+ (a plus)
CU L8R

RAF (rien a faire)
nufN2do (nothing to do)

2m1 (demain)
2moro

biz (bisous)
luv

06 (aussi)
2 (too)

How old are you?
T'as quel âge?
👄 ta kel azh

12 years old
Douze ans
👄 dooz on

Happy birthday!
Bon anniversaire!
👄 bon anee-versair

What's your star sign?
C'est quoi, ton signe astrologique?
👄 say kwa toh seen yastro-lojeek

When's your birthday?
C'est quand, ton anniversaire?
👄 say kon, ton anee-versair

Star signs

AQUARIUS
Jan. 21 – Feb. 19
le Verseau — lerver-so

PISCES
Feb. 20 – Mar. 20
les Poissons — lay pwason-so

ARIES
Mar. 21 – Apr. 20
le Bélier — ler belly-er

TAURUS
Apr. 21 – May. 21
le Taureau — ler tor-oh

GEMINI
May 22 – June 21
les Gémeaux — lay jem-oh

CANCER
June 22 – July 23
le Cancer — ler cancer

LEO
July 24 – Aug. 23
le Lion — ler lee-on

VIRGO
Aug. 24 – Sep. 23
la Vierge — la vee-erj

LIBRA
Sep. 24 – Oct. 23
la Balance — la ba-lons

SCORPIO
Oct. 24 – Nov. 22
le Scorpion — ler scorpion

SAGITTARIUS
Nov. 23 – Dec. 21
le Sagittaire — ler sajitair

CAPRICORN
Dec. 22 – Jan. 20
le Capricorne — ler capricorn

13

14

soccer le foot

🗣 ler foot

rollerblading
le roller

🗣 ler roller

music
la musique

🗣 la mew-zeek

electronic games
les jeux électroniques

🗣 lay jer ay-lek-tro-neek

tv
la télé

🗣 la taylay

comics
la BD

🗣 la bay-day

teddy bears
les nounours

🗣 lay noonoor

school l'école

🗣 lay-kol

spiders les araignées

🗣 layz aran-nyay

15

What's your favorite ...?

Quel est ton/ta ... préféré(e)?

💋 kel ay ton/tah ... preh-fairay

group
(ton) groupe
💋 (ton) groop

color
(ta) couleur
💋 (tah) koo-ler

Page 69

game
(ton) jeu
💋 (ton) jer

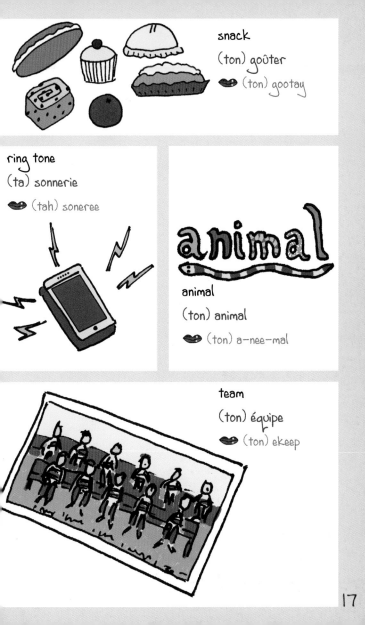

snack

(ton) goûter

(ton) gootay

ring tone

(ta) sonnerie

(tah) soneree

animal

(ton) animal

(ton) a-nee-mal

team

(ton) équipe

(ton) ekeep

17

Talk about your pets

He's hungry
Il a faim
eel ah fam

Can I pet your dog?
Je peux caresser ton chien
jer per karessay ton shy

She's sleeping
Elle fait dodo
el fay dodo

Do you have
any pets?
T'as des animaux
compagnie?
tah dayz anim
der kopanyee

cat

le chat

🗨 ler sha

dog

chien

🗨 ler shee–an

snake

le serpent

🗨 ler sir–pon

guinea pig

le cochon d'Inde

ler ko–shon d'and

hamster

hamster

🗨 ler amster

parakeet

la perruche

🗨 la peroosh

My Little doggy goes *oua-oua-oua!*

A French doggy (that's "toutou" in baby language) doesn't say "woof, woof," it says *"oua, oua"* (*waa-waa*). A French sheep says *"bêê, bêê"* (*bear-bear*) and a cluck-cluck in French chicken-speak is *"cot-cot"* (*ko-ko*). But cats do say "miaow" whether they're speaking French or English!

Talk about school (if you can bear it)

geography
la géo
👄 la jay-o

PE
la gym
👄 la jeem

art
le dessin
👄 ler dessa

French
le français
👄 ler fron-say

math
les maths
👄 lay mat

20

English
l'anglais
👄 lon-glay

music
la musique
👄 la mew-zeek

science
les sciences
👄 lay see-yons

history
l'histoire
👄 lis-twar

21

IT

l'informatique

🗣 lanfor-mateek

Way unfair!

French children have very long vacation breaks: 9 weeks in the summer and another 6–7 weeks throughout the rest of the year. But before you turn green with envy, you might not like the mounds of *"devoirs de vacances"* (*der-vwa der vacans*), that's "vacation homework!" And if you fail your exams, the teachers could make you repeat the whole year with your little sister!

Gossip

Can you keep a secret?

Tu peux garder un secret?

 too per garday er sekray

Do you have a boyfriend (a girlfriend)?

T'as un petit ami (une petite amie)?

 tah er pteet amee (oon pteet amee)

An OK guy/An OK girl

Un mec sympa/Une fille sympa

 er mek sampa/oon fee sampa

Way bossy!

Quel commandant!

 kel comon-don

He/She's nutty!

Il/Elle est dingue!

 eel/el ay dang

What a creep!

Quel râleur!

 kel rah-ler

You won't make many friends saying this!

Bug off!
Dégage!
👄 day-gaj

Shut up!
La ferme!
👄 la ferm

you're fed up with someone, and you want to say
something like "you silly …!" or "you stupid …!", you can
start with **"espèce de"** (which actually means "piece of …")
and add anything you like. What about …

Stupid banana!
Espèce de banane!
(espes der banan)

or …

Silly sausage!
Espèce d'andouille!
(espes don-dooy)

ke your pick. It should do the trick. You could also
/ **"espèce d'idiot!"** *(espes dee-dyo)*. You don't need a
anslation here, do you?

Saying goodbye

Here's my address
Voilà mon adresse

👄 vla mon adres

What's your address?
Tu m'donnes ton adresse

👄 too mdon ton adres

Come to visit me
Viens chez moi

👄 vya shay mwa

How do you say goodbye to a skeleton?

Bone Voyage!

28

Have a good trip!

Bon voyage!

 bon vwoy-arj

Write to me soon

Écris-moi vite

ekree mwa veet

Send me a text

Envois-moi un texto

onvwa-mwa er texto

Let's chat online

On chat sur internet

on "chat" syur internet

Bye!

Au revoir!

oh rev-wa

What's your email?

C'est quoi ton e-mail?

say kwa ton e-mail

つ□@3◇*@ん.com

WANNA PLAY?

l'élastique
👄 lelasteek

le ping-pong
👄 ler "ping pong"

le baladeur
👄 ler balad-er

le yo-yo
👄 ler yo-yo

le portable
👄 ler porta-bler

WANNA PLAY?

Do you want to play ...?

Tu veux jouer ...?

👄 too ver joo-ay

... foos-ball?

... au baby-foot?

👄 oh baby foot

... cards?

... aux cartes?

👄 oh kart

... on the computer?

... sur l'ordinateur?

👄 syur lordee-nater

... tic-tac-toe?

... au morpion?

👄 oh more-pyon

33

Care for a game of **cat** or **leap sheep**?!

In France, playing tag is called playing "at cat"—**à chat** (*asha*). Whoever is "it" is the cat—**le chat** (*ler sha*). And you don't play "leap frog," you play "leap sheep"—**saute mouton** (*sote moo-ton*). Have you ever seen a sheep leaping?

Can my friend play too?
Mon copain peut jouer aussi?
mo kopan per jooway oh-see

I have to ask my parents
Il faut que je demande à mes vieu?
eel foh ker jer daymon ah may vyer

Who dares?

You're it!
Touché!
👄 tooshay

Race you!
On fait la course?
👄 on fay la koors?

I'm first
C'est moi le premier
👄 say mwa ler pre-myay

Who's winning?

Qui c'est qui gagne?

💋 kee say kee gan-yer

Ready, steady, go!

A vos marques, prêts, partez!

💋 ah voh mark, preh, partay

Where's the finish?

Où est la ligne d'arrivée?

💋 oo ay la leen-yer

dreevay

I need a head start

J'ai besoin de prendre de l'avance

💋 jay buzwa der prondrer der la-vons

37

Electronic games

l'écran

🗣 lay-kra

le CD-ROM

🗣 ler say-day-rom

la souris

🗣 la soo-ree

le clavier

🗣 ler clavee-ay

le micro

🗣 ler meekro

les écouteurs

🗣 layz aykoot

Show me
Montre-moi
🗣 montrer mwa

What do I do?
Qu'est-ce que je fais?
🗣 kesker jer fay

Am I dead?
Ch'suis mort?
🗣 shwee more

Shoot-em-up!
Tue-les!
🗣 tew-lay

How many lives do I have?
J'ai combien de vies?
🗣 jay konbee-yah der vee

How many levels are there?
Y'a combien de niveaux?
🗣 yah konbee-yah de neevo

39

It's virtual fun!

Do you have WiFi?
T'as le WiFi?

😛 ta ler weefee

Send me a message.
Envois-moi un message.

How do i join?
Comment je m'inscris?

I'm not old enough.
Je suis pas assez grand.

I'm not allowed.
J'ai pas le droit.

I don't know who you are.
Je sais pas qui vous êtes.

my blog
mon blog
mo "blog"

my contacts
mes contacts
may kontakt

my photos
mes photos
may foto

videos
s vidéos
may vidayoh

music ma musique
ma mooseek

41

hockey
le hockey
💋 ler okee

gymnastics
la gymnastique
💋 la gymnasteek

ballet
le ballet
💋 ler ballay

basketball
le basket
💋 ler basket

and, of course, we haven't forgotten *"le foot"*...

43

soccer

cleats
les godasses
🔊 lay godas

soccer gear
les affaires de foot
🔊 layz afayr der foot

ref
l'arbitre
🔊 lar-beetrer

shin pads
les protèges-tibias
🔊 lay protej-tibya

Well played!
Bien joué
🔊 beeyah joo-way

Pass! Passe!
🔊 pas

44

defender
le défenseur
💋 ler dayfonsur

attacker
l'attaquant
💋 latakon

Foul!
Coup-franc!
💋 koo fron

Penalty!
Le penalty!
💋 ler paynalty

He pushed me!
Il m'a poussé!
💋 eel ma poo-say

Goal!
Goal!
💋 just say it!

46

Not like that!

Pas comme ça!

 pah kom sa

You cheat! Tricheur! (boys only)

Tricheuse! (girls only)

tree-sher/tree-sherz

I'm not playing anymore

Je joue plus

jer joo ploo

It's not fair!

C'est pas juste!

say pah joost

Stop it!

Arrête!

aret

47

Showing off

a handstand?

le poirier?

👄 ler pwa-riyay

Can you do ...

Tu sais faire ...

👄 too say fair

Look at me!

Regarde-moi!

👄 re-gard mwa

a cartwheel?

la roue?

👄 la roo

this?

ça?

👄 sa

Impress your French friends with this!

You can show off to your new French friends by practicing this tongue twister:

Ces six sausissons-ci sont six sous, ces six sausissons-ci sont très chers

say see soseeson see son see soo, say see eeson see son tray shair

(This means "If these six sausages cost six sous, these six sausages are very expensive.")

Then see if they can do as well with this English one:

"She sells seashells on the seashore, but the shells she sells aren't seashells, I'm sure."

49

For a rainy day

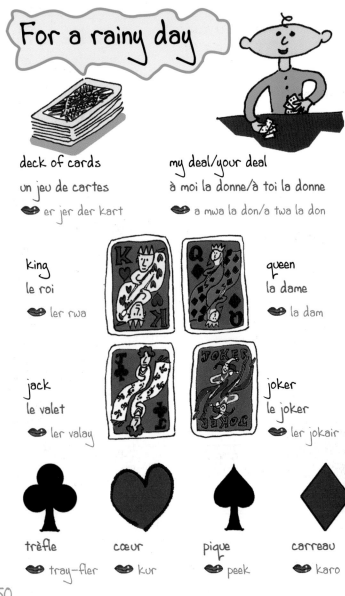

deck of cards

un jeu de cartes

💋 er jer der kart

my deal/your deal

à moi la donne/à toi la donne

💋 a mwa la don/a twa la don

king

le roi

💋 ler rwa

queen

la dame

💋 la dam

jack

le valet

💋 ler valay

joker

le joker

💋 ler jokair

trèfle

💋 tray-fler

cœur

💋 kur

pique

💋 peek

carreau

💋 karo

Grub (la bouffe)

I'm starving

J'ai une faim de loup

💋 jay oon fam der loo

That means "I have the hunger of a wolf!"

le loup

Please can I have ...

Donnez-moi, s'il vous plaît ...

💋 donay mwa, seel voo play

... a chocolate pastry

un pain au chocolat

... a croissant

un croissant

er krer-son

er pan oh shokolah

... an apple turnover

un chausson aux pommes

er show-son oh pom

... a chocolate eclair

un éclair au chocolat

er eklair oh shokolah

... a bun with raisins

un pain aux raisins

er pan oh rayzan

Chocolate eclair? *"Miam, miam!"*
Snail pancake? *"Beurk!"*
If you're going to make food noises,
you'll need to know how to do it
properly in French!
"Yum, yum!" is out in French.
You should say
"Miam, miam!" And
"Yuk!" is *"Beurk"* (pronounced "burk"),
but be careful not to let adults hear
you say this!

... a baguette

une baguette

💋 oon baget

... a pancake

une crêpe

💋 oon krep

... a waffle

une gaufre

💋 oon go-frer

Did you know?

A lot of children have hot chocolate for breakfast in the morning and some of them will dip their bread or croissants in it. It gets very soggy and Mom is sure not to like this!

Drink up

... I'm dying for a drink
... je meurs de soif
🗣 jer mur er swaf

I'd like ...
Je voudrais ...
🗣 jer voodray

... a coke
... un coca
🗣 er koka

... an orange juice
... un jus d'orange
🗣 er joo doronj

... an apple juice
... un jus de pommes
🗣 er joo der pom

57

... a lemonade

... une limonade

👄 oon leemonad

You can also have your lemonade with flavored syrup –then it's called "*diabolo*." The most well-known is "*diabolo menthe*," lemonade with mint syrup – hmmm!

... a syrup

un sirop

👄 er seero

... a milkshake

... un milkshake

👄 er meelkshek

You get your hot chocolate in a bowl (and that, at least, is a decent amount).

... a hot chocolate

... un chocolat

👄 er shokolah

A "crunchy man" sandwich, please

You never thought you could crunch up a man in France and get away with it, did you? Well, in France a grilled ham-and cheese sandwich is:

un croque-monsieur

👄 er krok murs-yur

… that means a "crunchy man." There's also a "crunchy woman!"

un croque-madame

👄 er krok ma-dam

… which is the same but with a fried egg on top.

Tails of snails

Did you know that snails have to be put in a bucket of salt water for three days to clean out their insides (don't ask!). After that they are baked in the oven in their shells and eaten with tons of garlic butter. And many French kids still love them!

Parties

French children often sing "Happy Birthday" in English when the candles are blown out on the cake. So you can practice singing the words with a French accent!

balloon la balle
💋 la bal

appee birzday too yoo!
appee birzday too yoo!

Can I have some more?
Je peux en avoir d'autre?
💋 jer per avwah door-trer

party hat
le chapeau cotillon
💋 ler shapoh koteeyon

This is for you
C'est pour toi
💋 say poor twa

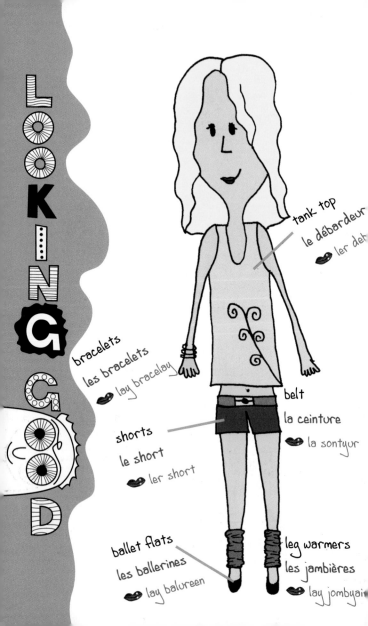

LOOKING GOOD

tank top
le débardeur
🫦 ler det

bracelets
les bracelets
🫦 lay bracelay

belt
la ceinture
🫦 la sontyur

shorts
le short
🫦 ler short

ballet flats
les ballerines
🫦 lay balureen

leg warmers
les jambières
🫦 lay jombyai

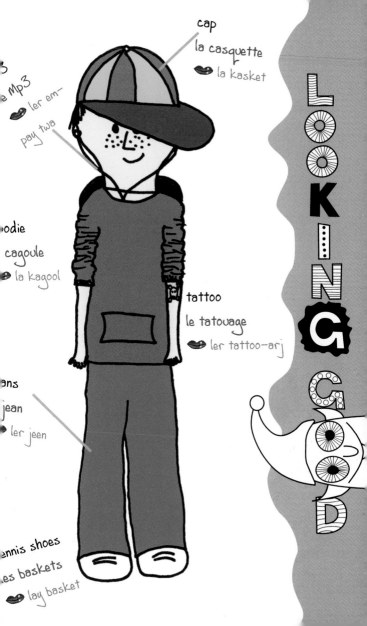

cap
la casquette
🗨 la kasket

3
e MP3
🗨 ler em-
pay twa

odie
cagoule
🗨 la kagool

tattoo
le tatouage
🗨 ler tattoo-arj

ans
jean
🗨 ler jeen

ennis shoes
es baskets
🗨 lay basket

LOOKING GOOD

Clothes

jeans
le jean
 ler "jean"

sweatshirt
le sweat
ler sw...

T-shirt
le T-shirt
ler "T-shirt"

soccer jersey
le maillot de foot
ler mayo der foot

tennis shoes
les baskets
lay basket

shoes
les chaussures
lay show–soor

64

dress
la robe
👄 la rob

skirt
la jupe
👄 la joop

pants
le pantalon
👄 ler panta-lon

Where's my pant?!

The French don't wear "pant**s**" or "jean**s**" – they wear only one of them: un pantalon (**er pantaloh**); un jean (**er jeen**). Strange, could've worn they had two legs!

65

That T-shirt, please
Ce T-shirt-là, s'il vous plaît
💋 ser "T-shirt" la, seel voo play

Cool tattoo!
Tatouage cool!
💋 tattoo-arj cool

The pink frilly one
Le rose à frous-frous
💋 ler roz a froo froo

The purple
striped one
Le violet à rayur
💋 ler vee-oh-la
a rayure

Awesome
miniskirt!
Minijupe d'enfer!
💋 minee-joop donfair

Where's my
skateboard?
Où est mon skate-board?
💋 oo ay mon "skateboard"?

66

spotted

à pois

👄 a pwa

flowery

à fleurs

👄 a fler

frilly

à frous-frous

👄 a froo froo

glittery

à paillettes

👄 a pie-et

striped

à rayures

👄 a rayure

Make it up!

lip gloss
le gloss
👄 ler gloss

glitter gel
le gel à paillettes
👄 ler jel a pie-yet

nail polish
le vernis à ongles
👄 ler vairnee a ongler

earrings
les boucles d'oreilles
👄 lay boo-kler doray

I need a mirror
J'ai besoin d'un miroir
👄 jay buzwa der mirwa

eye shadow
le fard à paupières
👄 ler fardah po-pyair

Can you lend
me your
flat iron?
Tu peux me prêter
ton fer à lisser?
👄 too per mer
pretay ton fair a leezay

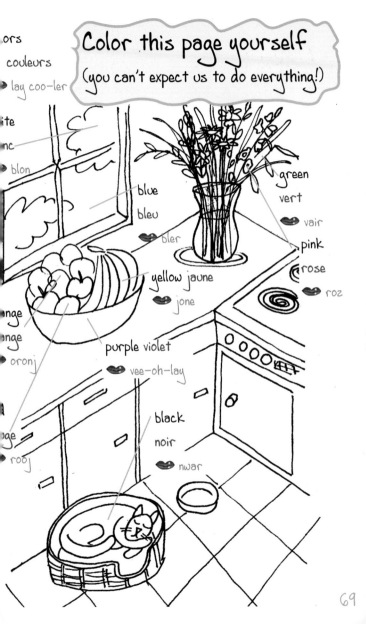

Color this page yourself
(you can't expect us to do everything!)

ors
couleurs
💋 lay coo-ler

ite
nc
💋 blon

blue
bleu
💋 bler

green
vert
💋 vair

pink
rose
💋 roz

yellow jaune
💋 jone

nge
nge
💋 oronj

purple violet
💋 vee-oh-lay

black
noir
💋 nwar

a
ge
💋 rooj

69

What should we do?

Qu'est-ce qu'on fait?

 kesk on fay

Can I come?

Je peux venir?

👄 jer per vuneer

Where do you all hang out?

Où traînez-vous?

👄 oo trainay voo

That's mega!

C'est géant!

👄 say jay-on

I'm (not) allowed

J'ai (pas) le droit

👄 jay (pa) ler drwa

Let's go back On y retourne

 onny rutoorn

That gives me goose bumps (or "chicken flesh" in French!)
Ça m'donne la chair de poule

 sa mdon la shair der pool

I'm bored to death
C'est mortel

say mortell

HOUSE OF MIRRORS

That's funny
C'est marrant

say maron

73

Beach bums

Can I borrow this?

Tu me prêtes ça?

too mer pret sa

Let's hit the beach

On va à la plage

on va a la plarj

Is this your bucket?

C'est ton seau?

say toh so

You can bury me

Tu peux m'enterrer

too per moterray

Stop throwing sand!

Arrête de jeter du sable!

arret der jetay dew sabler

Watch out for my eyes!

Attention à mes yeux!

attensee-on a maiz ye

beach la plage
🗨 la plarj

mer
🗨 la mair

ndcastle
château de sable
🗨 ler shato
r sabler

towel
la serviette
🗨 la sir-vee-et

bathing suit
le maillot
🗨 ler my-yo

bucket
le seau
🗨 ler so

shovel la pelle
🗨 la pel

orkel
tuba
🗨 ler tew-ba

shells
es coquillages
🗨 lay kokeeyarj

How to get rid of your parents and eat lots of chocolate!

In France there are great beach clubs that organise all sorts of games as well as competitions (sandcastles, sports, etc.). The prizes are often given by large companies who make kids' stuff such as chocolate and toys. Insist on signing up!

75

It's going swimmingly!

How to make a splash in French!

Let's hit the swimming pool

On va à la piscine

👄 on va a la piseen

Me too/I can't

Moi aussi/Moi pas

👄 mwa os-see/ mwa pa

Can you swim (underwater)?

Tu sais nager (sous l'eau)?

👄 too say najay (soo lo)

Can you dive?

Tu sais plonger?

👄 too say plonjay

I'm getting changed

Je me change 👄 jer mer shanj

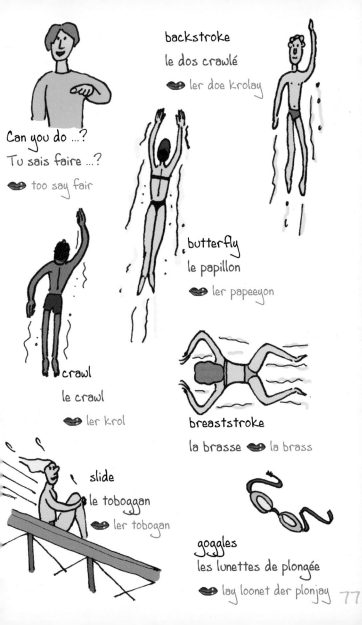

backstroke

le dos crawlé

🫦 ler doe krolay

Can you do ...?

Tu sais faire ...?

🫦 too say fair

butterfly

le papillon

🫦 ler papeeyon

crawl

le crawl

🫦 ler krol

breaststroke

la brasse 🫦 la brass

slide

le toboggan

🫦 ler tobogan

goggles

les lunettes de plongée

🫦 lay loonet der plonjay

77

Downtown

Do you know the way?
Tu connais le chemin?

👄 too konay ler shema

Let's ask
On va demander

👄 o va demonday

Pooper-scoopers on wheels!

You might see bright green-and-white motorcycles with funny vacuum cleaners on the side riding around town scooping up the dog poop. The people riding the bikes look like astronauts! (Well, you'd want protection too, wouldn't you?)

bus
le bus

👄 ler boos

Is it far?

C'est loin?

🗣 say lwan

Are we allowed in here?

On a le droit d'entrer ici?

🗣 on a ler drwa dentray eessee

car

la bagnole

🗣 la banyol

he "proper" French
ord for car is
oiture" (vwat-yure),
ut you'll look very
ncool saying this.
ick to "**bagnole**" (banyol), or if
e car is a wreck, try "**tacot**" (taco) for even more street
ed: "**Quel tacot**!" (kel tako—"What an old clunker!").

79

Park yourself here

swings la balançoire
🗨 la balonswar

jungle gym la cage à pou
🗨 la kaj ah pool

playground l'aire de jeu
🗨 lair der jer

grass l'herbe
🗨 lairb

tree l'arbre
🗨 larbrer

slide
le toboggan
🗨 ler tobogan

park le parc 🗨 ler park

Can we play ball games?
On peut jouer au ballon?
🗨 on per jooway oh balon

merry-go-round
le tourniquet
🗨 ler toornikay

sandbox
le bac à sable
🗨 ler bakah sabler

Can I have a turn? Je peux
essayer? 🗨 jer per esay-yay

Picnic (le pique-nique)

I hate wasps

Je déteste les guêpes

🗨 jer daytest lay gep

Move over!

Pousse-toi!

🗨 poos twa

bread

le pain 🗨 ler pan

Let's sit here

On s'assoie ici?

🗨 on saswa ees

napkin

la serviette

🗨 la sir-vee-et

ham le jambon

🗨 ler jambon

cheese

le fromage

🗨 ler frome

yogurt

le yaourt

🗨 ler ya-oort

chips

les chips

🗨 lay sheep

drinks
les boissons
🗣 lay bwason

knife
le couteau
🗣 ler koo-toe

spoon
la cuillère
🗣 la kwee-yeah

fork
la fourchette
🗣 la four-shet

wasps
les guêpes
🗣 lay gep

bees
les abeilles
🗣 layz abay

bzzzz

ants
les fourmis
🗣 lay foor-mee

83

Wake up, campers!

tent la tente
👄 la tont

tent peg
le piquet de tente
👄 ler peekay der t

camper van
le camping-car
👄 ler komping car

penknife
le couteau suisse
👄 ler kootoh swees

camping stove
le camping gaz
👄 ler komping gaz

sleeping bag le sac de couchage
👄 ler sak der kooshaj

flashlight
la lampe de poch
👄 la lomp
der posh

84

That tent's a palace!
Cette tente, c'est la classe!
💋 set tont, say la klas

Campfire
Le feu de camp
💋 ler fer der komp

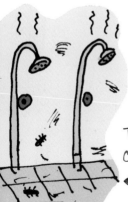

I've lost my flashlight
J'ai paumé ma lampe de poche
💋 jay pomay ma lomp der posh

These showers are gross
Ces douches sont crades
💋 say doosh son krad

Where does the garbage go?
Où est-ce qu'on jette les ordures?
💋 oo eskon jet layz ordyur

85

All the fun of the fair

slide

le toboggan

👄 ler tobogan

Ferris wheel

la grande roue

👄 la grond roo

house of mirrors

le palais des glaces

👄 ler palay day glas

bumper cars

les autos tamponneuses

👄 layz oto tomponerz

Let's try this

On essaie ça?

👄 on essay sa

octopus
le manège
🗨 ler manayj

It's (too) fast
Ça va (trop) vite
🗨 sa va (tro) veet

That's for babies
C'est pour les petits
🗨 say poor lay ptee

Do you get wet in here?
On sort mouillé d'ici?
🗨 on sor moo-yay deessee

I'm not going on my own
J'y vais pas tout seul
🗨 jee vay pa too surl

Disco nights

mirror ball
la boule multi-facettes
🗣 la bool multee-faset

loudspeakers
les enceintes
🗣 layz onsent

Can I request a song?
Je peux demander qu'on passe une chanson? 🗣 jer per dumonday kon pas oon shonso

The music is really lame
La musique est vraiment nulle
🗣 la mooseek ay vraymon nool

spotlights
les spots
🗣 lay spot

DJ
le DJ
🗣 lér "DJ"

mixing desk la tab de mixage 🗣 la tabler der meeksar

88

How old do I need to be?

Quel âge il faut avoir?

👄 kel aj eel foh avwah

dance floor

la piste de danse

👄 la peest der dons

Let's dance!

On danse!

👄 on dons

I love this song!

J'adore cette

chanson!

👄 jadoor set

honso

89

POCKET MONEY

candy
les bonbons
👄 lay bonbon

les T-shirts
👄 lay "T-shir

toys
les jouets
👄 lay joo-ay

le vendeur
👄 ler von-d

books

les livres

 lay lee-vrer

le mobile

ler mobeel

les crayons

lay crayon

Watch out! This means *pencils* NOT crayons!

POCKET MONEY

What does that sign say?

boucherie

butcher shop

🗣 booshree

pâtisserie

cake shop

🗣 pateesree

boulangerie

bakery

🗣 boolonjree

confiserie

candy store

🗣 konfeesree

papeterie

office supplies

🗣 paptree

épicerie

grocery store

🗣 aypeesree

boutique de vêtements

clothes shop

🗣 booteek der vetmon

Do you have some cash?
T'as des sous?
👄 tah day soo

I'm broke
Je suis fauché
👄 jer swee foshay

I'm loaded
J'ai plein d'sous
👄 jay pla dsoo

Here you go
Voilà
👄 vla

That's a weird shop!
Quel magasin bizarre!
👄 kel maguzah beezar

That's a bargain C'est pas cher
👄 say pa shair

It's a rip-off
C'est du vol
👄 say dew vol

93

Sweet heaven!

I love this shop

J'adore cette boutique

👄 jadore set booteek

Let's get some candy

On va acheter des bonbons

👄 on va ashtay day bonbon

Let's get some ice cream

On va acheter une glace

👄 on va ashtay oon glas

lollipops

des sucettes

👄 day sooset

a bar of chocolate

une tablette de chocolat

👄 oon tablet der shokola

chewing gum

chewing gum

👄 just say it, will you!

If you really want to look French and end up with lots of fillings, ask for:

des Carambars™ 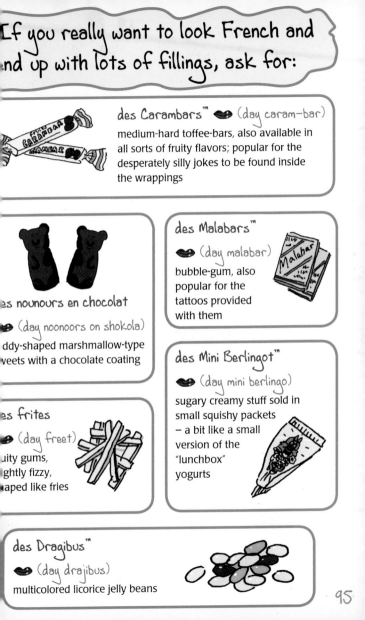 (day caram-bar)

medium-hard toffee-bars, also available in all sorts of fruity flavors; popular for the desperately silly jokes to be found inside the wrappings

des nounours en chocolat

(day noonoors on shokola)

teddy-shaped marshmallow-type sweets with a chocolate coating

des Malabars™

(day malabar)

bubble-gum, also popular for the tattoos provided with them

des frites

(day freet)

fruity gums, slightly fizzy, shaped like fries

des Mini Berlingot™

(day mini berlingo)

sugary creamy stuff sold in small squishy packets – a bit like a small version of the "lunchbox" yogurts

des Dragibus™

(day drajibus)

multicolored licorice jelly beans

Other things you could buy
(that won't ruin your teeth!)

What are you getting?
Qu'est-ce tu prends?
👄 keska too pron

That toy, please
Ce jouet là, s'il vous plait
👄 ser joo-ay la, seel voo p

Two postcards, please
Deux cartes postales,
s'il vous plait
👄 der kart
post-tal,
seel voo play

This is garbage
C'est nul
👄 say nool

This is cool
C'est cool
👄 say kool

I'm

getting ...

J'achète ...

 jashait

... a pen

un stylo

er stee-lo

... stamps

des timbres

day timbrer

felt-tip pens

s feutres

day fer-trer

... colored pencils

des crayons de couleur

day krayon der koolur

a key ring

porte-clés

er port

y

... comics

des BD

day bay day

... a fridge magnet

un aimant

💋 er aymon

... a shell box

une boîte à coquillages

💋 oon bwat ah kokeeyaj

... a necklace

un collier

💋 er kolyay

How much is that?

C'est combien?

💋 say kombee-yah

For many years France's favorite comics have been **Astérix** and **Tintin**. They have both been translated into English, as well as into many other languages. Today children also like to read:

Tom Tom et Nana
Boule et Bill
Natacha
Gaston Lagaffe

Money talks

How much pocket money do you get?

T'as combien d'argent de poche?

👄 tah komee-yah darjon der posh

I only have this much

J'ai seulement ça

👄 jay sulmo sah

Can you lend me
ten euros?

Tu peux me prêter
dix euros

👄 too per mer
pretay dee yooro

No way!

Pas question!

👄 pa kes-tyo

ʼney talk

nch money is the **euro** (pronounced *ew-roh*).
uro is divided into 100 **centimes** (*senteem*).
ns: 1, 2, 5, 10, 20, 50 **centimes**
      1, 2 **euros**
es: 5, 10, 20, 50, 100 **euros**
ke sure you know how much you are spending before
 blow all your pocket money at once!

Something has dropped/broken

Quelque chose est tombé/cassé

 kel-ker shose ay tombay/kassay

Please

S'il vous plaît

seel voo play

Can you help me?

Vous pouvez m'aider?

 voo poovay mayday

Where's the mailbox?

Où est la boîte aux lettres?

oo ay la bwat oh lettrer

Where are the toilets?

Où sont les toilettes?

102 oo son lay twalet

I can't manage it

Je n'y arrive pas

💋 jer nee arreev pah

Could you pass me that?

Vous pouvez me passer ça?

💋 voo poovay mer passay sa

What time is it?

Quelle heure il est?

💋 kel ur eelay

Come and see

Venez voir

💋 venay vwar

May I look at your watch?

Je peux voir sur votre montre?

💋 jer per vwar syur votrer montrer

Lost for words

... my ticket

mon billet

👄 mo beeyay

I've lost ...

J'ai perdu ...

👄 jay perdew

... my phone

mon portable

👄 mo portabler

... my parents

mes parents

👄 may paron

... my shoes
mes chaussures

👄 may sho-syur

... my money mon argent

👄 mo arjon

... my sweater
mon pull

👄 mo pool

... my watch
ma montre

👄 ma montrer

... my jacket ma veste

👄 ma vest

105

Adults only!

Show this page to adults who can't seem to make themselves clear (it happens). They will point to a phrase, you read what they mean, and you should all understand each other perfectly.

Ne t'en fais pas
Don't worry

Assieds-toi ici
Sit down here

Quel est ton nom et ton prénom?
What's your name and surname?

Quel âge as-tu?
How old are you?

D'où viens-tu?
Where are you from?

Où habites-tu?
Where are you staying?

Où est-ce que tu as mal?
Where does it hurt?

Est-ce que tu es allergique à quelque chose?
Are you allergic to anything?

C'est interdit
It's forbidden

Tu dois être accompagné d'un adulte
You have to have an adult with you

Je vais chercher quelqu'un qui parle anglais
I'll get someone who speaks English

107

EXTRA STUFF

weather
le temps
👄 ler toh

numbers les nombres 👄 lay nomb

time

l'heure

👄 lur

EXTRA STUFF

There was an English cat called "one, two, three" and a French cat called "un, deux, trois" standing waiting to cross a river. Both were afraid of water, so the English cat suggested that they race across to make it more fun. Who won?

Answer: "One, two, three"
because "un, deux, trois"
CAT SANK!

1 un 👄 un

2 deux 👄 der

3 trois 👄 twa

4 quatre 👄 katrer

5 cinq 👄 sank

6 six 👄 sees

ept 🗨 set

uit 🗨 weet

euf 🗨 nerf

dix 🗨 dees

onze 🗨 onz

douze 🗨 dooz

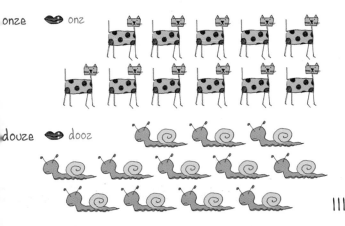

13 treize  trez

14 quatorze 👄 catorz

15 quinze 👄 kanz

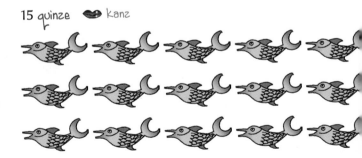

seize	*sez*	**19**	dix-neuf	*dees-nerf*
dix-sept	*dees-set*	**20**	vingt	*van*
dix-huit	*dees-weet*			

---

f you want to say "twenty-two," "sixty-five," and so on, you can just put the two numbers together like you do in English:

2	vingt-deux	*van der*
5	soixante cinq	*swasont sank*

nis works except if you're saying "twenty-one," "sixty-ne," and so on. Then you need to add the word for "and" t) in the middle:

1	vingt et un	*vant eh un*
1	soixante et un	*swasont eh un*

---

trente	*tront*
quarante	*karont*
cinquante	*sankont*
soixante	*swasont*
soixante-dix	*swasont dees*
quatre-vingts	*katrer van*
quatre-vingt-dix	*katrer van dees*
cent	*sonn*

a thousand   mille   *meel*

a million   un million   *er mil-yo*

billions and billions!   des milliards de milliards!
day meelyar der meelyar

The French must be really big on sums! Everything's fine until you reach 70. Instead of saying "seventy," they say "sixty-ten" (**soixante-dix**) and keep counting like this until they reach 80. So 72 is "sixty-twelve" (**soixante douze**), 78 is "sixty-eighteen" (**soixante dix-huit**), and so on.

Just so it doesn't get too easy, for 80 they say "4 twenties!" And to really make your brain ache they continue counting like this until a hundred. So 90 is "4 twenties 10" (**quatre-vingt-dix**), 95 is "4 twenties fifteen" (**quatre-vingt-quinze**) … you remembered your calculator, didn't you??

March	mars	*mars*
April	avril	*avreel*
May	mai	*meh*

June	juin	*joo-wah*
July	juillet	*joowee-eh*
August	août	*oot*

eptember	septembre	*septombrer*
October	octobre	*octobrer*
November	novembre	*novombrer*

December	décembre	*desombrer*
anuary	janvier	*jonvee-eh*
ebruary	février	*fevree-eh*

printemps *prantom*

été *eteh*

automne *awtom*

AUTUMN

hiver *eever*

WINTER

Monday	lundi	*lundee*
Tuesday	mardi	*mardee*
Wednesday	mercredi	*mecredee*
Thursday	jeudi	*jurdee*
Friday	vendredi	*vendredee*
Saturday	samedi	*samdee*
Sunday	dimanche	*deemonsh*

By the way, French kids don't usually have school on Wednesdays, but they have to go on Saturday mornings. Still – that's half a day less than you!

Good times

It's ...
Il est ...
👄 eel ay

(one) o'clock
(une) heure
👄 (oon) ur

quarter after (two)
(deux heures) et quart
👄 (der zur) ay kar

quarter to (four)
(quatre heures) moins le quart
👄 (katr ur) mwan ler kar

half past (three)
(trois heures) et demie
👄 (twa zur) ay demee

five after (ten)

(dix heures) cinq

👄 (dees ur) sank

twenty after (eleven)

(onze heures) vingt

👄 (onz ur) van

ten to (four)

(quatre heures) moins dix

👄 (katr ur) mwan dees

twenty to (six)

(six heures) moins vingt

👄 (sees ur) mwan van

morning
matin

🫦 ma-tah

midday
midi

🫦 meedee

afternoon
après-midi

🫦 apray meedee

evening soir

🫦 swar

midnight
minuit

🫦 meenwee

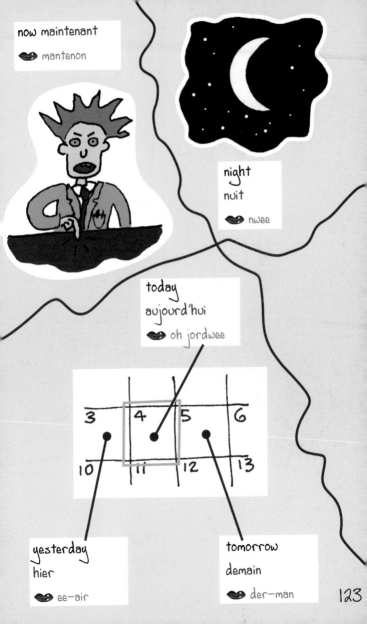

now maintenant
👄 mantenon

night
nuit
👄 nwee

today
aujourd'hui
👄 oh jordwee

3 4 5 6
10 11 12 13

yesterday
hier
👄 ee-air

tomorrow
demain
👄 der-man

123

Weather wise

Can we go out?
On peut sortir?

👄 on per sorteer

It's hot
Il fait chaud

👄 eel fay show

It's cold
Il fait froid

👄 eel fay frwa

It's horrible
Il fait mauvais

👄 eel fay movay

It's raining ropes!

In French it doesn't rain "cats and dogs," it rains "ropes!" That's what they say when it's raining really heavily:
Il pleut des cordes
eel pler day kord

It's windy
Il fait du vent
👄 eel fay dew von

It's sunny
Il fait du soleil
👄 eel fay dew solay

It's raining
Il pleut
👄 eel pler

It's snowing
Il neige
👄 eel nej

I'm soaked
Je me suis fait tremper
👄 jer muswee fay trompay

It's nice Il fait beau
👄 eel fay bow

125

Signs of life

Taille Minimum

Minimum Height

Eteindre les téléphones

Turn off your telephone

Entrée Interdite

No Entry

Interdit aux moins de dix-huit ans

Under 18s not allowed

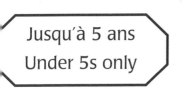

Jusqu'à 5 ans
Under 5s only

HORS-SERVICE

OUT OF ORDER

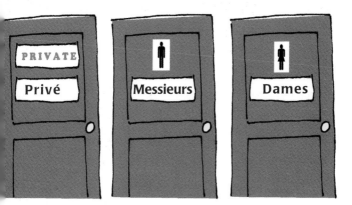

PRIVATE

Privé

Messieurs

Dames